They Came Together In Bethlehem

Messages For
The Advent/Christmas Season

Thomas A. Pilgrim

The Beholders
written by
Lisa Johnson

CSS Publishing Company, Inc., Lima, Ohio

THEY CAME TOGETHER IN BETHLEHEM

Copyright © 1999 by
CSS Publishing Company, Inc.
Lima, Ohio

Scripture quotations are from the *Revised Standard Version of the Bible*, copyrighted 1946, 1952 ©, 1971, 1973, by the Division of Christian Education of the National Council of the Churches of Christ in the USA. Used by permission.

Library of Congress Cataloging-in-Publication Data

Pilgrim, Thomas A., 1944-
    They came together in Bethlehem : messages for the Advent/Christmas season / Thomas A. Pilgrim.
        p.   cm.
    ISBN 0-7880-1512-5 (pbk. : alk. paper)
    1. Advent sermons. 2. Christmas sermons. 3. Children's sermons. 4. Methodist church Sermons. 5. Sermons, American. 6. Worship programs. I. Title.
BV4254.5.P55   1999
252'.612—dc21   99-37625
                                                                                                        CIP

This book is available in the following formats, listed by ISBN:
        0-7880-1512-5   Book
        0-7880-1513-3   Disk
        0-7880-1514-1   Sermon Prep

PRINTED IN U.S.A.

*This book is dedicated to the following people
whose friendship, encouragement, and example
have come together to enrich my life and ministry*

*Rev. Howard Bledsoe
Rev. Terry Phillips
Rev. Greg Porterfield
Rev. Derrick Rhodes
Rev. George Sedberry
Dr. Gordon Thompson*

Table Of Contents

Preface

There is no other place like Bethlehem. It is the place of our Savior's birth. That makes it unique among all the towns and cities of this world.

The first Christian Roman Emperor was Constantine. He legalized the Christian faith all across the empire. His mother, Helena, soon traveled to the Holy Land, and located the site of the birth of Jesus in Bethlehem, the site of his resurrection in Jerusalem, as well as other important places. She had churches built on these sites. The one in Bethlehem was dedicated in the year 339. This church was destroyed in 521, and the current one was built in 531. When the Crusaders came to this church they lowered the size of the door so no one could ride horses inside any longer. Now when one goes there, one must bow down in order to enter.

In February of 1998 I visited Bethlehem for the seventh time. Each time I go there I am impressed by the fact that people from all over the world come together in Bethlehem. As I thought about this on one of my trips there I realized it is not just people who come together in Bethlehem. Many things come together in Bethlehem. The great purposes of God come together in Bethlehem. As we sing, the hopes and fears of all the years come together in Bethlehem. And for all of us, life comes together in Bethlehem because of what happened there on a cold, dark night when a star lit up the sky and God's love warmed the hearts of a few people who came together in Bethlehem.

It was on that trip when I thought about everything coming together in Bethlehem that I first began to visualize this series of sermons. I shared them with my congregation, and now I share them with a wider audience.

This series contains something new. When I was pastor at St. John United Methodist Church in Atlanta, Georgia, Ms. Lisa Johnson, a young lady in our congregation, shared with me some dramatic readings she had written. These are called "The Behold-ers." I used them at my current church with these sermons. The persons presenting them were dressed in costume, which helped to bring alive the people in this drama of the first Christmas. Lisa Johnson is a creative writer who left a position with a national ad agency to enter the ministry. She graduated from Candler School of Theology, Emory University, in Atlanta, Georgia, and is a can-didate for ministry in the United Methodist Church. I want to thank her for letting me use these readings in my church and in this book.

I also want to thank my wife Shirley for her encouragement in the ministry of preaching and writing. I owe her a debt I could never pay.

Thomas A. Pilgrim

They Came Together In Bethlehem:
The Prophetic Word —
And The Living Word

Years ago I ran across the following story. I am not sure where I read this, but I have never forgotten it.[1]

At the end of time all the people who had ever lived came together to be judged by God. They were all complaining and talking very loudly. There were all sorts of people there, and many of them had been treated very cruelly. They were angry and bitter over the treatment they had received.

There was a group of Jews who had suffered under the Nazis, and a group of black slaves. There were people from all over the world who had suffered at the hands of others. There were people who had lived before the flood and after the bomb — before Christ and after Freud. And all of these people who felt they had suffered unjustly began to question God's right to judge them, since he had never suffered the kind of treatment they had received. They all decided that before God could judge them he would have to suffer what they had been through.

So they began to pronounce their sentence. They said, "Let him be born a Jew. Let the legitimacy of his birth be questioned. Give him a work so difficult even his family will think him mad when he tries to do it. Let him be rejected by the very people who worship him. Let him be betrayed by his dearest friends. Let him be indicted on false charges, and tried before a prejudiced jury, and convicted by a cowardly judge. At last, let him see what it is like to be terribly alone and completely abandoned by his friends. Let him be tortured. Then let him die."

As each person pronounced his sentence loud cries of approval went up from the crowd. When the last sentence was pronounced

9

there was a long silence. Those who were there began leaving quietly. No one uttered a word. They suddenly realized that God had already served his sentence. "The Word became flesh and dwelt among us."

Today is the First Sunday in Advent. This is the season of preparation which leads us to the celebration of the birth of Jesus Christ. During the Advent season we will think together about the theme, "They Came Together In Bethlehem." We begin with this: "The Prophetic Word — And The Living Word."

In Bethlehem people of all colors, cultures, creeds, races, religions, and languages come together. It is just a country town near a big city. But people from all over the world come together in Bethlehem. It has always been so.

Many things come together in Bethlehem. Not just people but also the great purposes of God. Converging upon Bethlehem were people and events which would change the world forever.

The hope of it, the dream of it, the vision of it began much earlier in the faith of God's people and in the words of God's prophets who spoke God's words of deliverance. The one who spoke most clearly what God would do about saving his people was Isaiah. He more than any other person spoke of the coming of the Messiah to deliver God's people, to save them. Here in chapter 40 he writes: "Comfort, comfort my people, says your God. Speak tenderly to Jerusalem, and cry to her that her warfare is ended, that her iniquity is pardoned, that she has received from the Lord's hand double for all her sins. A voice cries: 'In the wilderness prepare the way of the Lord, make straight in the desert a highway for our God.' " Then, further down in this passage we read, "Get you up to a high mountain, O Zion, herald of good tidings ... say to the cities of Judah, 'Behold your God!' "

Then, in the opening of the Gospel according to Saint John, this prophetic word comes together with the living word as John proclaims, "The Word became flesh and dwelt among us, full of grace and truth; we have beheld his glory, glory as of the only Son from the Father."

So John opens his gospel with this great sweeping statement about the Son of God coming into the world and living among us.

This is the fulfillment of the longings of a people and the promises of God to them.

The prophetic word and the living Word came together in Bethlehem. And we come together in Bethlehem. It is there that we all come together and find the meaning of our living. Life comes together in Bethlehem.

Look at the elements in this great event which enable us to discover life.

I

First, there is the mystery of incarnation. That is the first thing we discover here in these words of Saint John.

He opens his Gospel with the same phrase which begins the Book of Genesis, "In the beginning ... In the beginning was the Word, and the Word was with God, and the Word was God. He was in the beginning with God; all things were made through him, and without him was not anything made that was made."

When John uses the term "the Word" he is referring to God himself. The Greek term is *Logos*, meaning the creative presence of God's power. God spoke into creation all that is. Everything comes from God's spoken word.[2] And John says, "The Word became flesh." God's creative power has come into the world as a person — God's Son, Jesus Christ.

The incarnation is the greatest fact in the history of the world. "Incarnate" means a clothing, to put on. God put on humanity and became one of us.

This is a mystery. It is not something we can explain. But it is something we proclaim. So in these early days of Advent prepare yourself, that you may proclaim the mystery of incarnation.

Some parents wanted to be sure their children understood Christmas. They were concerned because one of their children was constantly asking for a watch he wanted at Christmas. He asked for that watch 312 times a day. Finally, they told him to cool it. And they decided to tell their children to come to the breakfast table on Saturday morning with a memorized Bible verse about Christmas. Their daughter quoted hers proudly: "John 3:16: For God so loved the world that he gave his only begotten Son." Then their oldest son said, "John 1:14: The Word became flesh and dwelt among us." Finally, the youngest son said, "Matthew 24:42: What I say to you I say to all, watch!"

Watch and be ready to proclaim the mystery of incarnation.

There was a new baby in the family and they all went to the hospital to see him. At first they only saw him in the nursery through the great glass window. But the three-year-old sister could not see very well. Then he was brought to his mother's hospital room. But there were too many relatives passing him around. Finally the big sister protested, "When can I get close enough to see his face?"

This is what the mystery of incarnation has done, for "the Word became flesh and dwelt among us."

There is something more we see here.

II

Second, there is the meaning of identification. That is the next thing John tells us.

He writes, "He was in the world, and the world was made through him, yet the world knew him not. He came to his own home, and his own people received him not."

He came into the world and identified himself with his own people. He became one of them.

When Saint Paul writes about this to the Philippians he uses the term *kenosis*, meaning "to empty." He says, he "emptied himself, taking the form of a servant, being born in the likeness of men. And being found in human form he humbled himself and became obedient unto death, even death on a cross."

Here in these opening words of his Gospel John sets the stage for all that is to come. He tells us about the meaning of the life of Jesus Christ, who identified himself with the people of the world, and he gave himself to them, even to the point of dying for them.

The identification of Christ with us is the most compelling fact in the history of the world. The meaning of this event brings salvation to the world and to us. This is God's wonderful gift to us, his children.

A woman had gotten caught up in the last few days of the Christmas rush. Thinking all her shopping was done, she realized

12

on Christmas Eve she had not mailed any Christmas cards. She rushed to the store and bought a box of fifty cards. She signed them hastily, addressed them and took 49 of them to the post office. She came back home, sat down in the den for a moment and looked at the one left over and read these words: "This card is just to say a little gift is on the way." She rushed back out to buy 49 gifts and get them on the way.

This great gift of Christ's identification with us is a gift we can share.

In a little book called *The Gift Of Christmas*, a lady named Mary Janes tells of going to church on Christmas Eve. Eight months earlier the funeral of her husband had been held there. As she waits for the service to begin, a little girl comes down the aisle, looking for a seat. Mary motions for her to come sit on her pew. The beautiful service ends with the singing of "Silent Night." Mary's eyes fill with tears, as she thinks of past Christmas Eves. As she holds a handkerchief to her mouth, the little girl's hand takes Mary's hand and squeezes it. And Mary's heart is filled with joy.[3]

Perhaps you could share the gift of identification and the gift of Christ with someone this Christmas.

III

The next thing John tells us is that there is the miracle of imitation.

Even though the world did not know him or accept him, and even though his own people did not accept him, "to all who received him, who believed in his name, he gave power to become children of God; who were born, not of blood nor of the will of the flesh nor the will of man, but of God."

Those who receive the Son of God become the children of God. They become like him. The imitation of Christ is the highest form of life in the history of the world. Centuries ago Thomas à Kempis wrote a book called *The Imitation of Christ*. Jesus asked those who followed him, "Be imitators of me."

This is a miracle. Aside from the miracle of the birth of Christ and the miracle of the resurrection of Christ this is the greatest miracle, that we could become the children of God, become like him.

13

This is a miracle which takes place in our lives. It is something we live. This miracle changes our perspective, our minds, our opinions, our habits, our hopes, our dreams, our goals, our living.

This is a miracle which can take place every Christmas. It is not just the miracle of the birth of Christ. It is also the miracle that can take place in you and me at Christmas.

James W. Moore relates a story told by Dr. Fred Craddock. It is the story of a missionary named Oswald Golter. His mission board called him home from China because of World War II. They sent him the money for a ticket. On his way home he had to wait at a port in India to make connection with his ship. He met there some stranded refugees, with no place to go. They were being kept in a warehouse. Since it was Christmas he wished them a Merry Christmas. He then asked them what they wanted for Christmas. They told him they were not Christians and did not believe in Jesus. He said, "I know, but what do you want?" They finally told him about some German pastries they liked. He cashed in his ticket and searched all over the city until he found them. He bought several baskets full and gave them to the refugees. Much later on he told this story to some students. One of them asked, "Why did you do that for them? They weren't Christians. They don't even believe in Jesus." Oswald Golter said, "I know, but I do."[4]

Because the prophetic word and the living Word came together in Bethlehem, we have a faith that is proclaimed — we proclaim the mystery of the incarnation. We have a faith that is shared — we share the meaning of identification. We have a faith that is lived — we live the miracle of imitation.

Thanks be to God!

---

1. I have been unable to locate the source of this story.

2. Gail R. O'Day, "The Gospel of John," *The New Interpreter's Bible, Volume IX* (Nashville: Abingdon Press, 1995), p. 519.

3. Mary Janes, "The Touch Of A Hand," *The Gift Of Christmas*, by Jayne Bowman (Norwalk, Connecticut: The C. R. Gibson Company, 1987), p. 25.

4. James W. Moore, *Standing On The Promises Or Sitting On The Premises* (Nashville, Tennessee: Dimensions for Living, 1995), p. 80.

Lighting Of The First Advent Candle

Leader: Scripture Reading — Isaiah 40:1-5

Leader: This candle we light today reminds us of the light of Hope the prophets had in their expectation of a Messiah who would bring God's love to the world.

People: Come, Lord Jesus, come.

Prayer

O God, as we begin this Advent season we enter thy courts with praise and thy gates with thanksgiving, and we lift up these ancient doors that the King of glory may come in.

Enable us to prepare our hearts to receive anew the birth of thy Son and our Savior, Jesus Christ. Help us to make room in our lives for his life.

We thank thee, gracious Father, for all thy blessings upon us. For the abundance of good things we have, the wealth of opportunity that is ours, the richness of our faith, the worth of our lives, the value of our relationships we thank thee, O God. Enable us to share these blessings with those who have little or nothing.

Fill our hearts and minds in this season with songs of faith and joy. Lift our hopes beyond despair and put a new note of victory in our living.

Be especially with those who have great burdens, illness, sorrows, and be the great physician for them.

Bless all the great people of the world. May all of us welcome to the world the Prince of Peace, the Hope of the world, the Son of the Most High God, for we pray in his name. Amen.

Looking At Our Chrismons:
A Scroll

Boys and girls, I am so glad you have come to worship today on the First Sunday in Advent.

Advent is a time when we prepare for the coming celebration of the birth of Jesus. One of the ways we do this is by putting up our Chrismon tree. A Chrismon is really a Christ-monogram. It is a symbol which teaches us something about Jesus Christ. On each of the Sundays during the Advent and Christmas seasons I want to talk with you about one of these.

The first one we look at today is a scroll. Who knows what this is? That's right. It is an old book. Both the Old and New Testaments were first written down on scrolls like this. They were rolled up and then unrolled to be read.

Each Sunday one of our scripture lessons will be from the Old Testament book Isaiah.

Isaiah was a prophet. He spoke for God. And he was the one who, more than any other, talked about the coming of the Messiah. This would be a person who would save God's people.

Jesus Christ is that person. In fact, the word "Christ" means "Messiah." Jesus is the one God sent to be the savior of the world.

When we see the scroll on our Chrismon tree we are reminded this is who Jesus is and what he came to do.

Let us pray together. O God, we thank you for the words of hope from Isaiah about the coming of Jesus. And we thank you for the gift of Jesus. We pray in his name. Amen.

The Prophet

Since Jacob, since Abraham, since the angels took up their watch at the Gates of Eden, God's people have waited for the Messiah. The prophets of old spoke of a leader who would bring the sons and daughters of Israel out of sin, a king born of David's line. He would reign for all time, of his kingdom there would be no end. Could this child in Bethlehem really be the one?

The prophecies say that our Savior shall be born in humble circumstances. This place is below humble — it's disgusting. Dirty, smelly, no place for a woman to be having *any* child, let alone the Son of God. Angels surround this unholy shed, and those three regal-looking men have brought impressive gifts indeed. But the rest of this crowd is quite common. Why, those shepherds are still dusty from the fields, and look, the woman who runs the inn — she's hardly a pious woman. Stonecutters, weavers, fishermen, farmers, dancers — oh, no, even the prostitutes are here. Well, if we are to look for humble, this is certainly humble.

But the Messiah is to be wise and powerful. *This* Messiah is only a baby helpless in his mother's arms. Look at them. His mother is not much more than a girl! And his father is an ordinary man, a carpenter. See how they are attended by the cattle in the stalls!

And yet, look at these people. They have come not to see the star or hear the angels, but to bow before this child. They are somber. They are reverent. Yes, they are worshiping. Look at that old shepherd, barely able to walk without his grandson's help. Yet he's down on his creaky old knees, his wrinkled face shining like a boy's. And that rough-edged innkeeper, she offers a tender gift to this tiny king: the first tears she's shed in years.

I am in the presence of miracles. People come into his presence and are changed. They are freed from their pasts, they are given hope and life, they are made whole. By their faith in this infant Messiah, they are saved.

And so I speak *my* prophecy. He will come humbly to the dark and dirty stable in your heart. Some will turn away; some will make room for him. Receive him! And the empty manger in your soul will be filled with his light.

They Came Together In Bethlehem:
The Hope Of A Girl —
And The Hope Of The World

Years ago in a small European town a visitor noticed that on one of the streets when the citizens of the town walked by a certain wall they would nod and make the sign of the cross. As he stood there and watched he observed that they all did this. He became curious about the practice and began to ask around. But no one could tell him what it meant. Finally, he obtained permission to investigate the wall. He began to chip away layers of paint and dirt. He discovered underneath them a beautiful mural of Mary and her baby. People had always made the sign of the cross as they passed by that painting even after it was covered over. They had passed on the tradition, though the reason for it had been lost.[1]

Remove some of the things in which we dress Christmas and there beneath the surface you come to the central meaning of it. And you find there this beautiful story about a young girl and her baby — the hope of a little girl and the hope of the world.

On these Sundays we are thinking together about the theme, "They Came Together In Bethlehem." And today we turn to this: "The Hope Of A Girl — And The Hope Of The World."

Long ago the prophet Isaiah saw a time when God would send a Messiah to set his people free. We read earlier that passage in which God speaks to King Ahaz, telling him to ask for a sign. But Ahaz responds by saying, "I will not ask, and I will not put the Lord to the test." Isaiah answers for God, saying, "Hear then, O house of David! Is it too little for you to weary men, that you weary my God also? Therefore the Lord himself will give you a sign. Behold, a young woman shall conceive and bear a son, and shall call his name Immanuel." That name means "God with us." That would be a sign that God would save his people.

Centuries pass by and finally the hope of the world comes through the hope of a girl. Saint Luke tells us about it. The angel Gabriel was sent by God to a little out-of-the-way town up in the Galilee district. He spoke a simple message to a simple peasant girl. Her name was Mary. She was just a teenage girl, whose future had already been planned for her by her family and the family of a man named Joseph, a carpenter by trade. But God had other plans for Mary. He chose her to be the mother of the Messiah.

God chose her because she was only engaged, and there would be no doubt this virgin was having God's Son and the son of no other. But we know people, don't we? And we know what they said about her. However, she and Joseph held onto what the angel Gabriel had said about him: "Do not be afraid, Mary, for you have found favor with God. And behold, you will conceive in your womb and bear a son, and you shall call his name Jesus."

It is here in this event that we see coming together in Bethlehem the hope of a girl and the hope of the world.

Young Mary, approaching marriage, had wonderful hopes about her own little family and the birth of her own little children. Her hopes came together with God's plan about his Son who would be born to become the hope of the world.

The hope of this girl has become the hope of the world — and he is our only hope. This is what the Advent season says to us. Prepare to receive the hope of the world.

The commentary on this passage in Luke in the *New Interpreter's Bible* was written by Alan Culpepper, Dean of the Theology School at Mercer University in Atlanta, Georgia. He said, "The glory of Christmas came about by the willingness of ordinary people to obey God's claim on their lives."[2]

I wonder if you are willing to do that, to obey God's claim on your life? If you are you will experience the glory of Christmas, and you will find hope in your life, the hope of the world.

I want to tell you why this child became the hope of the world.

I

He is the hope of the world because he is God coming to us.

Gabriel said to Mary, "He will be great, and will be called the Son of the Most High." He is God coming to us. He is bringing God into our world and our experience.

We have him as a part of our lives today and will forever. That is what this Advent time of preparation is all about. We are getting ready to celebrate the fact that he is God coming to us.

There is a story I love to tell at Christmas. A pastor traveled from his church in a small town to a large city. While there he was to purchase a sign to go on the lawn of his church during the Advent season. He had both the words and the dimensions written down on a piece of paper, but when he arrived he realized he had forgotten to bring it with him. He sent a telegram to his wife, "Send motto and dimensions." It was during the lunch break and a different clerk was on duty when the reply came back. She fainted and fell on the floor when she read it, for the message said, "Unto us a child is born, six feet long and two feet wide."

A child has come to us. I wonder if you really believe this for yourself. Is it really true for you?

A professor went through an hour-long lecture on the existence of God. Finally, he turned to one of his students and said, "Now have I proved to you that there is a God?" The young man replied, "You didn't have to prove it to me. I knew it all along."[3]

I wonder if you really believe this for yourself. I wonder if you not only believe this intellectually, but if you would also be willing to receive it. Would you believe it and receive it?

A woman had a sick child and was unable to get her any help. She read in the paper about a famous doctor being in town. She prayed he would come to her house. Out for a walk that afternoon, the doctor was caught in the rain. He knocked on her door, but she refused to open her door and let him come inside. She refused to believe God was answering her prayer.[4]

God sent his Messiah to his people. They had been asking for and looking for him for a long time. But when he arrived the vast majority of them refused to open their doors to him.

21

Sometimes we say, "Oh God, come help me!" But I wonder.

In this Advent season I hope you will remember he is the hope of the world and your only hope, because he is God coming to us.

II

He is the hope of the world because he is God ruling over us.

Gabriel said to Mary, "The Lord God will give to him the throne of his father David." He not only comes to us, he is God ruling over us. We have him taking part in our lives today and will forever.

That is what this Advent time of preparation is all about. We are getting ready to celebrate the fact that the one who has come will rule over us.

Do you really believe this for yourself? Is it really true for you?

One time in *Peanuts* Lucy said to Charlie Brown, "Merry Christmas! Since it is Christmas, I think we ought to bury the hatchet and put our past differences behind us and try to be kind!" Charlie Brown thinks it's a great idea, and says, "Why does it have to be limited to Christmas? Why can't it be all year long?" She looks at him and says, "What are you, some kind of fanatic?"[5]

How far are you willing to go with all this Jesus stuff? Are you willing not only to believe Jesus is God ruling over us, but also to receive his rule in your life, and over your life?

When Josef Stalin came to power in Russia he destroyed the Cathedral of Christ the Savior. In its place he was having built the monument to the Soviet Union, with a great statue of himself on top. But as it was being built it began sinking into the ground. The weight of it was too great to hold up. The city of Stalingrad no longer bears his name. Jesus Christ remains, but where is Stalin now?

With what are you filling your life? What kind of monument are you building? Monuments we build to ourselves are always too heavy to hold up. They sink in the ground. Those which show God is ruling over us always remain firm.

Some tourists in Brazil came to a place where they could see that great statue of the Christ of the Andes. But the clouds moved

22

in and suddenly they could no longer see it. Their guide said to them, "It's all right. He'll be there when the clouds move away."[6]

In this Advent season I hope you will remember he is the hope of the world and your only hope because he is God ruling over us. And I hope you will let him always be there, ruling over you.

III

Finally, he is the hope of the world because he is God including us.

Gabriel said to Mary, "He will reign over the house of Jacob forever; and of his kingdom there will be no end." He not only comes to us and rules over us, he is also God including us. We are a part of that kingdom today and will be forever. We are included and always will be.

That is what this Advent time of preparation is all about. We are getting ready to celebrate the fact that the one who has come has included us forever.

Do you really believe this for yourself? Is it really true for you? Are you willing not only to believe Jesus is God including us, but to be included and to accept your inclusion in his kingdom, of which there will be no end?

Edgar Dewit Jones was a well-known preacher in earlier years. One night at the end of a service a man came down the aisle and took the hand of Reverend Jones. He said, "Preacher, you said God could save anybody, no matter who they were or what they had done. I want to believe that. I want him to save me." Then he told all the things he had done and said, "I'm a Swedish blacksmith by trade ... I don't know whether God can help me or not." Edgar Dewit Jones said, "You are in luck. God is specializing in Swedish blacksmiths tonight!"[7]

Whoever you are, God has included you. You are his specialty.

I hope you will remember in this Advent season Jesus is the hope of the world and your only hope, because he has included you. Sometimes he is the only one who does. I hope you will always be included.

In her book *Kneeling in Bethlehem*, Ann Weems says: "You see what concerns me, what lies on my heart, is this: that we in the church papered and programmed, articulated and agendaed, are telling the faith story all wrong, are telling it as though it happened 2,000 years ago or is going to happen as soon as the budget is raised. We seem to forget that Christ's name is Emmanuel, God with us, not just when he sat among us but now, when we cannot feel the nailprints in his hand."[8]

He is with us now — God is coming to us, God ruling over us, God including us.

He is not just the hope of a girl. He is the hope of the world. Our only hope.

Thanks be to God!

----

1. James W. Moore, *Standing On The Promises Or Sitting On The Premises* (Nashville, Tennessee: Dimensions For Living, 1995), p. 32.

2. R. Alan Culpepper, "The Gospel Of Luke," *The New Interpreter's Bible, Volume IX* (Nashville, Tennessee: Abingdon Press, 1995), p. 53.

3. John Killinger, *The Greatest Teachings Of Jesus* (Nashville, Tennessee: Abingdon Press, 1993), p. 26.

4. Earl G. Hunt, *A Bishop Speaks His Mind* (Nashville, Tennessee: Abingdon Press, 1987), p. 177.

5. William J. Carl III, *Waiting For The Lord* (Nashville, Tennessee: Abingdon Press, 1988), p. 60.

6. *Emphasis* (Lima, Ohio: CSS Publishing Company, issue unknown), p. 17.

7. Moore, *op. cit.*, p. 80.

8. Ann Weems, *Kneeling In Bethlehem* (Philadelphia, Pennsylvania: The Westminster Press, 1980), p. 75

Lighting Of The Second Advent Candle

Leader: Scripture Reading — Isaiah 7:10-14

Leader: This candle we light today reminds us of the light of Salvation the prophets had in their expectation of a Messiah who would redeem God's people.

People: Thanks be to God.

Prayer

Eternal God, Father of all humankind, who has sent thy well-beloved Son to be the Hope of the world, so prepare our hearts in this season of Advent that we would be able to receive him and have our lives filled with hope.

We thank thee, O God, for all thy blessings upon us, for we know thou art the source of every good gift. We thank thee for all the ways thou hast blessed us, for the gift of life, for strength and faith and courage, for work to do, for people who care about us.

We are thankful for this Advent season, and for him whose birth we celebrate. May he find a rebirth in us so that in our lives we would reflect the meaning of who he is.

Fill our hearts with love, and put a new song on our lips. Enable us to give, to share, to rejoice, to dream. Fill our thoughts and motives and deeds with peace and joy and good will.

Continue to bless us, O God, with the knowledge of thy presence. Continue to lead us as a church, and work thy good work in us and through us that thy Kingdom may know no boundaries.

Bless the sick of our church family and those who are troubled, and we will give to thee all honor, praise, and glory, for we pray in the name of the Prince of Peace. Amen.

Looking At Our Chrismons:
A Cross

Good morning, boys and girls. Who knows what today is? That's right. It's the Second Sunday in the season of Advent. Remember, this is the time of preparing for the celebration of the birth of Jesus.

On these Sundays we are talking about our Chrismons. A Chrismon is a Christ-monogram.

Today I want to talk with you about this one. We have several of these on our tree. Why do you think we have crosses on our tree here at Christmas? That's right, because Jesus was born so that he could live in this world and then finally die on a cross and be resurrected. He overcame the cross and death and the tomb.

This was a part of God's plan for his life all along.

When Mary was told she was going to have a baby she was also told to name him Jesus, for he would save his people from their sins. He would be great and would be the Son of God.

Jesus came into the world to save his people — to save the world. He is still today the hope of the world.

That is why the cross is a symbol of hope for us. We not only have it on our tree, we also have it other places here in our church. It is on our altar table. Many of us wear crosses around our necks.

The cross at one time was a symbol of suffering and death. Now it stands for victory and life and hope. This is true because Jesus is the hope of the world.

Let us bow our heads for our prayer. O God, our Father, we thank you for your Son and our Savior, Jesus Christ. We pray in his name. Amen.

Mary, The Mother

(*Aside, to Joseph*) Wrap the cloth a little tighter, dear, the baby might be cold.

(*To audience*) No woman is ever ready for motherhood, I suppose. But I was just getting used to being betrothed. With marriage staring me in the face, I thought I was as terrified as I could get. Then one night the angel came and told me what was to happen to me. I thought, "No, no, you've made a mistake. I'm much too young to bear the Messiah. Please, God, choose someone older, someone stronger, better, someone ... *else*."

(*Aside*) Joseph, please cover his face. It's dusty in here.

(*To audience*) But I saw the beauty of God's plan — God's son, coming to share life with all of us, life as *we* live it, dirt, tears, and all. The Son would be born of an ordinary woman, like any other baby. And I'm certainly ordinary. Well, maybe God sees something sacred in being ordinary. Maybe from now on, all the ordinary people will feel especially blessed by God.

I thought all that over, and I said yes to God's plan, and I haven't had a moment's peace since. Oh, no. You'd think saying yes to God would put you in some kind of peaceful, restful state. Don't misunderstand, I do feel like the most blessed of women, and I also believe that I'm part of something so big and so eternal. But peaceful? Just the opposite. Now I have to live up to God's faith in me. Now I have a stake in being a better person, because that baby boy is counting on me and Joseph. I'm a mother now. I'm Jesus' *mother.*

(*Aside*) Let me hold him now, Joseph. I think he's hungry.

(*For the rest of the monologue, Mary speaks to the baby in her arms*) I wish I knew what your life will be like. The savior of all people for all times. Will you be the mighty hero, leading the children of Israel to great power? Or will you save them quietly, ruling their souls instead? Will you have a loving wife at your side, and sons and daughters of your own, and grandchildren one day? Or will you have a few faithful friends to make your life's journey with you? If only I could protect you, my little Jesus, if only I knew what was in store for you, maybe I could keep you safe, surround you with love and happiness and ... But that's not for me to decide, is it? Your life belongs to God. Mine too.

The King of kings. And born in this dark, dirty stable. You don't look like a king. You look like a baby boy. God lifts up the lowly, my son. Believe it.

Third Sunday In Advent
Isaiah 11:1-10; Luke 2:1-5

They Came Together In Bethlehem:
The Expectant Parents —
And An Unexpected Baby

Some time ago I read a story in a church newsletter written by a pastor in Tennessee. He told about his congregation's being in a new sanctuary for their first Christmas there. It was going to be a great Advent Sunday. The choir had put in extra time working on their music. He had prepared a sermon on "The Unexpected God." The church was full that Sunday, and the service began with the singing of "Hark! The Herald Angels Sing." Just as the affirmation of faith ended, a boy announced from the back of the church, "Mr. Bob Buford's house is burning down!" Mrs. Buford, who was in the choir, fainted and fell. They revived her, and she and some firemen rushed to the fire. The congregation tried to settle down and continue the service. But suddenly a woman came in and said, "The whole town is burning up!" The preacher pronounced the benediction, and everyone ran out the door. Only one house burned after all. That afternoon the preacher thought about all this, and knew the effort to help a person was more important that the music and the sermon. He remembered too how the first Christmas took place in the midst of human suffering, and how, "When no one was looking, our unexpected God slipped in among us and changed the world forevermore."[1]

That is the way God does things. People in those days long ago in that land far, far away looked for God in the Temple. But the unexpected God appeared in the hay of a dirty stable in a little country town.

On these Sundays we are thinking together about the theme, "They Came Together In Bethlehem." Now we look at this: "The Expectant Parents — And An Unexpected Baby."

29

In ages past the prophet Isaiah wrote about the coming of the Messiah. He told how he would grow out of the family tree of David, Israel's greatest king. He would not judge by what he saw, but with righteousness he would judge the poor and decide with equity for the meek. And because of him a new time would be ushered in when "the wolf shall dwell with the lamb, and the leopard shall lie down with the kid, and the calf and the lion and the fatling together, and a little child shall lead them."

Then we come to this passage in the Gospel of Luke where we find this simple story unfolding. Today we look at only the first five verses, which tell us briefly that when Augustus was the emperor of Rome there was a census. The people went back to their own hometowns to register. Joseph and Mary went from Nazareth to Bethlehem, "The House of Bread," the home of David, because Joseph was from that long family tree. Mary was expecting a baby.

Alan Culpepper writes in *The New Interpreter's Bible* that it is significant that Saint Luke gives us this very brief account, after having spent all of chapter 1 writing about Elizabeth and Mary. But this brief account tells us what everybody knew. Augustus had brought peace to the Roman Empire. However, it is Jesus the Savior who brings "peace on earth, good will to men."[2]

It is through the lives of these expectant parents that God does the unexpected with this unexpected baby.

Nobody in those days expected anything of a baby. They respected power. The Romans perfected power. They inflicted power. That is why they had the *Pax Romana*, the peace of Rome. Nobody was able to fight them.

Nobody in those days expected anything of Bethlehem. It was just another little country town in an out-of-the-way province of Rome. But it is to this town these expectant parents journey.

Then we see coming together in Bethlehem these expectant parents and the great purposes of God in this unexpected baby.

It is through this unexpected baby that God sends us what we need. It is the gift of Christmas. We see God's gifts to us coming together in Bethlehem.

I

First, this unexpected baby brings unexpected power. He brought the power of God into this world of human experience.

Luke tells us this baby was born when the emperor of Rome was Caesar Augustus. He was the symbol of power in the world. The power of Rome was present throughout all the empire. But here is this baby bringing into this world an unexpected power — the power of God.

For the next three centuries those who followed the one born in Bethlehem were persecuted and executed. The power of Rome came down hard on them. But then after 300 years an unexpected thing took place. A young army general named Constantine was converted and became a Christian. He had his soldiers paint a cross on their shields. And under the sign of the cross, he took over the empire and became the emperor. His mother Helena traveled to the Holy Land to find the place where Jesus was born in Bethlehem, and she had a church built over that place. Christianity was legalized, and the empire became known as the Holy Roman Empire. What an unexpected turn of events.

God has sent us the gift of power.

Jesus promised his disciples and us, "You shall receive power."

During a Christmas pageant a little girl was playing the part of one of the angels. It came time for her to say her line, "Glory to God in the highest...." But she forgot the rest of it. She tried it again, and still could not remember. She tried again and came out with, "Glory to God in the highest ... and I'll huff and I'll puff and blow your house down!"

That is not the power God sends. It is a different kind of power. We find this power in unexpected ways and in unexpected places for unexpected uses. It is the power of God which he sends upon us, gives us, which enables us to be his servants, his witnesses, and his people. It is a power which enables us to endure, to keep on going, to go through times of suffering and times of danger. It is a power which enables us to respond to life in Godlike ways.

On a trip to the Holy Land we went to the Holocaust Museum in Jerusalem. There is a tree there which was planted in memory of Oscar Schindler, the man who saved the lives of so many Jews in

31

the Nazi death camps. I stood there by that tree and thought about the movie *Schindler's List*. At one point in the story Schindler talks with a Nazi officer who tells him he has the power to exterminate a person. But Schindler says to him, "That is not power. Anyone could do that. But to have a man come before you and to say, 'I could take your life if I so choose, but no — instead, I pardon you!' That, Commander, is power!"

We have been given the power to live Godlike lives in Godlike ways, not to destroy, but to create; not to tear down, but to build up; not to seek for ourselves, but to serve.

This unexpected baby brought unexpected power.

II

Second, this unexpected baby offers unexpected peace. He brought the peace of God into this world of human experience.

Luke tells us also this baby was born when Quirinius was governor of Syria. All of those Roman provinces had governors who were there for one reason — to keep the peace. But here is this baby bringing into this world an unexpected peace — the peace of God. The peace of Rome was imposed upon everyone. But the peace of God was offered to everyone.

God has sent us the gift of peace. That is the song of the angels — "Glory to God in the highest, and on earth peace among men with whom he is pleased." Jesus said, "My peace I give to you." Saint Paul wrote, "The peace of God passes all understanding."

Though this peace is available to us we do not always possess it. Sometimes we miss it.

In his book, *Christmas Gifts That Always Fit,* James W. Moore tells about a man who lived in Athens, Georgia. While waiting for a bus he saw a machine which, for 25 cents, would tell him his name, age, hometown, and other information. He decided to try it. He put in the quarter and the machine said, "You're Bill Jones. You are 35. You live in Athens. You are waiting for the bus to Greenville, South Carolina. It is delayed." He thought that was incredible and decided to try it again, and got the same answer. But the machine told him the bus was delayed a little longer. Then he decided to fool the machine. He went across the street to a store and bought some of those glasses with the mustache and eyebrows. He came back and put in another quarter. The machine said, "Well, it's you again. You are still Bill Jones. You live in Athens. You are 35 years old. You want to go to Greenville, South Carolina. But while you were horsing around, you missed your bus!"[3]

Sometimes we miss the peace of God. We miss it because we look for it in the wrong way in the wrong place for the wrong kind of peace. We find this peace of God in unexpected ways and in unexpected places for unexpected uses. It is the result of responding to life in Godlike ways.

Father William J. Bausch tells of the man who always has a special feeling each year when he receives his first Christmas card. It reminds him of the lady who lived next door when he was growing up. She was 95 years old. Often he would deliver to her the groceries his mother would buy for her. One day during Christmas he went over to take the groceries and she gave him the usual tip. But he decided not to accept it this time. She insisted that he take it. He sat there for a long time and talked with her. She told him about her early life, their country church, and Christmas. Finally, when he left her house he went across the street to the store. He could buy a lot of candy with the tip she gave him. But then he thought of her and how alone she was. He decided to buy her a Christmas card, and he searched through the cards looking for just the right one. Then he saw it. It had on the front a country church just like the one she had told him about. He bought the card, signed his name to it, and took it back over to her house. When she came to the door, he held it out and said, "Hello, Mrs. Hildebrand. Merry Christmas." She began to cry, thanked him, and wished a Merry Christmas to him. A few weeks later she died in her sleep. Her night-table light was on. On the table there stood the Christmas card he had given her. It had brought some joy into her life.[4]

We are given the peace of God which comes from living in Godlike ways, sharing the peace of Christ.

This unexpected baby brought unexpected peace.

III

Third, this unexpected baby is an unexpected person. He brought the person of God into this world of human experience.

Luke tells us that during this time of Caesar Augustus and Quirinius a man named Joseph went from Nazareth to Bethlehem with his wife Mary, who was expecting a baby. Here is this baby bringing into the world an unexpected person — the person of God. The person of God is shared with all the world, "For God so loved the world that he gave his only begotten Son, that whosoever believes in him should not perish, but have everlasting life."

God has sent us the gift of a person. He comes to us himself.

We find this person in unexpected ways and in unexpected places for unexpected reasons. God meets us along the way, makes himself known to us, and invites us to give our lives to him.

Albert Schweitzer wrote these words about him:

> He comes to us as One unknown, without a name, as of old, by the lakeside, he came to those men who knew him not. He speaks to us the same word: "Follow thou me!" and sets us to the tasks which he has to fulfill for our time. He commands. And to those who obey him, whether they be wise or simple, he will reveal himself in the toils, the conflicts, the sufferings which they shall pass through in his fellowship, and as an ineffable mystery, they shall learn in their own experience who he is.[5]

Martin Luther was preaching during the Christmas season, describing what it must have been like for Joseph and Mary and this baby, and how much help they needed. He said to his listeners that maybe they were thinking they would have done something had they been there then. "Well, do it now," Luther said, "for there are people all around us. Do something for him now."[6]

Paul Tillich wrote about the Nazi war crimes trials. During those proceedings a story was told about some Jews hiding out in a cemetery. They slept in the graves at night. One night a young woman gave birth to a baby boy in one of those graves. He was delivered by an eighty-year-old gravedigger. When the baby cried out the gravedigger held him up in his hands and said, "Great God, hast thou finally sent the Messiah to us? For who else than the Messiah himself can be born in a grave?"[7]

We have been given the person of God. The Messiah was born in a manger. He leads us to live in Godlike ways, to do Christlike things and to do them for him.

When we give our lives to him we discover unexpected power and unexpected peace and we even live like this unexpected person.

Thanks be to God!

---

1. Ron D. Williams, "First Church Informer," First United Methodist Church, Millington, Tennessee, June 22, 1994.

2. R. Alan Culpepper, "The Gospel of Luke," *The New Interpreter's Bible, Volume IX* (Nashville, Tennessee: Abingdon Press, 1995), p. 63.

3. James W. Moore, *Christmas Gifts That Always Fit* (Nashville, Tennessee: Dimensions For Living, 1996), p. 75.

4. William J. Bausch, *Storytelling The Word* (Mystic, Connecticut: Twenty-third Publications, 1996), p. 209.

5. Albert Schweitzer, *The Quest For The Historical Jesus* (New York: Macmillan, 1950), p. 403.

6. Moore, *op. cit.*, p. 18.

7. Paul Tillich, *The Shaking Of The Foundations* (New York: Scribner's Sons, 1948), p. 165.

Lighting Of The Third Advent Candle

Leader: Scripture reading — Isaiah 11:1-10

Leader: This candle we light today reminds us of the light of Peace
the prophets had in their expectation of a Messiah who
would bring peace to the world.

People: Praise be to God.

Prayer

O God, our Heavenly Father, the creator of all that is, the sustainer
of life, who also participates in it with the coming of thy Son, Jesus
Christ, into the world, we call upon thee today to hear our prayers
and to accept the worship and praise we give to thee.

We thank thee, Father, for the greatest gift, the gift of thy Son
and our Savior King. May we open our hearts and lives to him, and
may he find a place to live in us.

We thank thee, O God, for the gracious ways thou hast been at
work in our lives, for thou has delivered us, sustained us, strength-
ened us, and has caused our lives to overflow with good things.
For all that life is we thank thee, O God.

We thank thee for the church of Jesus Christ, for this church
and the dedicated people who serve the cause of Christ through the
mission and ministry of this church.

Continue to bless us with the leadership of thy Spirit, and lead
us all to service, mission, and witness.

Bless all in our church and community who suffer from illness, sorrow, burdens, ignorance, deprivation. Bring healing, help,
wholeness, and make us the instruments of thy peace.

And we pray in the name of him who came to be all things to
all people. Amen.

Looking At Our Chrismons:
A Manger

Good morning. I am so glad to see all of you here today. It is now what Sunday in Advent? That's right. It's the Third Sunday. We are moving right along, and soon Advent will be over.

On these Sundays I am talking with you about the Chrismons on our Chrismon tree. A Chrismon is what? Yes, it is a Christ-monogram, and it tells us something about Jesus Christ.

Today we look at this one. It is a manger. Our scripture lesson today tells us that Joseph and Mary went on a long trip to Bethlehem. They got there late at night and could not find a place to stay. The only place they could find was in a barn where animals were kept. It was really a cave carved out of the side of a hill. And a manger was a place which held hay. The animals ate the hay out of the manger.

This manger on our Chrismon tree helps us remember this about Jesus. It reminds us that he was born to be our King and Savior and that he came into the world in a humble place, a lowly place.

We still sing about that today as we sing "Away In A Manger."

Whenever you look up at our Chrismon tree and see a manger there, remember where Jesus was born — in a low place, because God sent him down to be with us. And he became one of us. He was not born in a palace, into wealth and power. He was born in a place which was a shelter for animals. Because of that we find shelter in him.

Let us pray. Father in Heaven, thank you for sending your Son down to us. We pray in his name. Amen.

Joseph

Our firstborn is a son.

I look at him, all wrapped in cloth, sleeping in Mary's lap. The angels have told us he is the Son of God. But he is *my* son, too. He has his mother's eyes, but he has his father's hands. Those tiny hands are destined for the wood and nails of the carpenter's trade.

I am committed to his destiny, this son of ours. But I don't yet know what part I am to play. God chose Mary and me to raise this holy child. God even sent an angel to convince me to be Mary's husband. And the angel told *me* to name the baby "Jesus." But I've had no more messages since the angel came many months ago. Mary has given Jesus life. What shall *I* do?

I look forward to teaching him carpentry. Mary says I am the finest carpenter in Nazareth. And I do love my trade. Each wood is unique in color and texture, each one special, from the beautiful cedar to the amazing mustard, an herb, really, but it grows as tall as a tree from the smallest of seeds. But, am I to teach Jesus about trees? What divine destiny is there in knowing trees?'

Is my Jesus the one to lead the people of Israel? If such a leader would help us conquer our fear, then he must know fear, too, and learn courage. If he is to bring strength to the weary and sorrowful, then he must have his own heart broken and learn to let love heal it. He must dwell among us, and understand us, and live his life fully as a man. That is my part, then. God needs me to show my little boy how to be a man.

And so I will. Sweat and hard work will make him strong; laughter and tears will deepen him. When he is happy, he will sing; when he is frightened, he will reach out for help. He will learn to be a true and faithful friend, to trust and to love. His faith will grow, and he will come to know his heavenly Father as well as he knows me.

I give him my whole heart, my life, everything I have to give. I will feed him and clothe him, teach him, protect him. If I have to, I will die for him.

God is his heavenly Father, but I am his papa.

They Came Together In Bethlehem:
The Song Of Angels —
And The Son Of God

Samuel Beckett wrote a play called *Waiting For Godot*, waiting for God. It is a two-act play in which two men stand on stage. The only thing there with them is a tree with no leaves. One of the men speaks to the other, trying to talk to him about two thieves on a cross and one being saved. But the other man will not talk about that. In the second act there are a few leaves on the tree. One of the men becomes excited because he thinks Godot is coming. But they never see him. At the end of the play they decide they will kill themselves unless he comes. One says, "And if he comes?" The other replies, "We'll be saved!"[1]

There are people still waiting for God, hoping to find him, see him, hear him, discover him, invent him, always waiting, hoping, wondering. But you need look no further than Bethlehem.

In a church's Christmas pageant a little boy had the part of an angel, and he was to say, "I bring you good news of great joy." But he could not remember the line. So he burst out with, "Boy, have I got some good news for you!"[2]

I have some good news for you. We need look no further than Bethlehem.

During this Advent season we have been thinking together about the theme, "They Came Together In Bethlehem." Today we look at "The Song Of Angels — And The Son Of God." We see coming together in Bethlehem the great purposes of God in the song of angels and the Son of God.

Centuries earlier the prophet Isaiah wrote those words which told of his arrival: "The people who walked in darkness have seen a great light; those who dwell in a land of deep darkness, on them

41

has light shined. Thou hast multiplied the nation, thou hast increased its joy ... For to us a child is born, to us a son is given; and the government shall be upon his shoulder, and his name will be called 'Wonderful Counselor, Mighty God, Everlasting Father, Prince of Peace.' "

Last Sunday we read about a man named Joseph and his young wife Mary coming down to Bethlehem town. We read a little further in this story today. We learn from Saint Luke that "while they were there, the time came for her to be delivered."

That baby was born in a barn because there was no other place for them to stay. It was a place for animals, cut out of the side of a sandstone hill. Imagine that, the Son of God coming down to this earth not in a palace of honor, but a place of humility; not in the seat of power, but the site of poverty; not in a circle of influence, but a city of insignificance.

Then Saint Luke tells us, "In that region there were shepherds out in the field, keeping watch over their flock by night. And an angel of the Lord appeared to them, and the glory of the Lord shone around them, and they were filled with fear. And the angel said to them, 'Be not afraid; for behold, I bring you good news of a great joy which will come to all the people.' "

Here we see coming together in Bethlehem the song of angels and the Son of God.

Did you get it? Did you hear it? The song of angels is all about "good news of great joy for all people." Do you know who that means, who it includes? It is for us. The song of the angels and the Son of God came together in Bethlehem for us.

So here on this Sunday before Christmas let me remind us of some basic things for us to remember, to hang on to, to live by and live for.

I

First, the Savior is here for us. This is the Good News of great joy at Christmas. The Savior is here for us.

That was the message of the angel, and it is for us. "For to you is born this day in the city of David a Savior, who is Christ the Lord."

Make this up-close and personal for yourself, and know deep down in your heart the Savior is here for all the world and for you.

I remember the most moving sermon I ever preached. It was the Sunday before Christmas. There was a lady in our church expecting a baby any day. About halfway through my sermon she went into labor. And the ending of my sermon was so stirring that at 1:15 that afternoon a bouncing baby boy was born. That is Christmas up-close and personal! He was here.

When our youngest child was born we thought she was arriving on Christmas Eve. But then she waited a little longer and finally was born two days after Christmas. That is why we named her Christie. That is Christmas up-close and personal! She was here.

Make Christmas up-close and personal for you. Because a Savior is here for us, life takes on a new meaning and is lifted to a higher level. It will never be the same.

The Savior saves us from this world of sin and suffering and death. He puts us in touch with God. He brings us the Good News of God's love for us his children. He transforms the meaning of our existence.

Open your hearts to welcome the Savior. Let him find a place to live in you.

One little boy played the part of the innkeeper in his church's Christmas pageant. When the holy family knocked on his door he said, "No, go away. There is no room in the inn." But they persisted, and he gave the same answer. Still they persisted. Finally, he said, "Oh, okay. You can have my room."

The Savior is here for us. Let him find room with you.

Move further along and let me remind you of this.

II

Second, the sign is given for us. This is the good news of great joy at Christmas. The sign is given for us.

That was the message of the angels, and it is for us. "This will be a sign for you: you will find a babe wrapped in swaddling cloths and lying in a manger."

Make this up-close and personal for yourself, and know deep in your heart the sign is given for all the world and for you.

Make Christmas up-close and personal for you. This is the sign — a child lying in a manger. It is something we understand.

God comes to us in the stuff of life, not in some theory, not in a complicated set of rules to live by, not in any otherworldly philosophy, not in some mystical trance, but in something we can relate to.

A little boy got a treehouse for Christmas. When he and his dad began putting it together, they discovered the directions were for a treehouse, but the parts were for a sailboat. The very next day Dad wrote a letter of complaint. He received an immediate reply. It read, "We are sorry about the error. But it might help you to think about the man somewhere out on a lake trying to sail a treehouse."[3]

This world would make religion so complicated, but it is really simple. God is not some great theory or set of directions. This child is a sign of who he is, what he is like, what he will do. This is where we find him. We find him in lowly things, in the common things, in a barn, in a feed trough, in the hay, among lowly people. This sign is given for us. Claim it for yourself.

A Sunday school teacher led her children to create a manger scene. Each Sunday during Advent they would add to it the characters. But toward the end of the season the teacher noticed one little girl seemed concerned about it, so she asked her if anything was wrong. The little girl replied, "Where will we find Jesus in all of this?"

> *To be himself a star most bright*
> *To bring the wise men to his sight*
> *To be himself a voice most sweet*
> *To call the shepherds to his feet*
> *To be a child — it was his will,*
> *That folk like us might find him still.*[4]

The sign is given for us. Find him for yourself.

III

Third, the song is sung for us. This is the good news of great joy at Christmas. The song is sung for us.

That was the message of the angels, and it is for us. "And suddenly there was with the angel a multitude of the heavenly host praising God and saying, 'Glory to God in the highest, and on earth peace among men with whom he is pleased.' "

Make this up-close and personal for yourself, and know deep down in your heart the song is sung for all the world and for you.

Make Christmas up-close and personal for you. This song is for us. But it must also be sung by us. We are the ones who must carry it on and do the singing. We must be the ones who share this good news.

In order to do that we must remember this is our Savior, our sign, our song.

William Faulkner wrote a story called "Tomorrow." It was televised on PBS years ago. Robert Duvall played the part of Jackson Fentry, a cotton farmer who worked in the winter as the caretaker of a sawmill. He lived there in the boiler room. One night a woman expecting a baby comes to his door. She has no place to go. He invites her in and takes care of her. Her baby is born in that place. Fentry worked all night making a crib, and he takes it in to her. He sits down by the bed, looks at them, and says, "Can I hold the baby?" She hands him over. She knows she is going to die, so she says to Fentry, "Will you take care of him if I die?" He answers, "Yes." Then she asks, "Like he is your very own?" He replies, "Yes."

Will you take care of him like he is your very own? He is, you know. He was born for you.

A family brought home a new baby. He cried a lot that first night. The new mother read through the pages of a baby book trying to find just what to do. Finally, her mother said to her, "For heaven's sake, Sarah, put down the book, and pick up the baby!"[5]

You pick up the baby. He is yours, up-close and personal.

The Savior is here for you. The sign is given for you. The song is sung for you and by you.

Thanks be to God!

---

1. John Killinger, *The Salvation Tree* (New York: Harper & Row Publishers, 1973), p. xiv.

2. Wallace D. Chappell, *The Trumpet's Certain Sound* (Nashville, Tennessee: Wallace Chappell Ministries, Inc., 1987), p. 17.

3. James W. Moore, *Christmas Gifts That Always Fit* (Nashville, Tennessee: Dimensions For Living, 1996), p. 52.

4. Charles L. Allen and Charles L. Wallis, *Christmas*, "Childhood" by John Erskine (Old Tappan, New Jersey: Fleming H. Revell Company, 1977), p. 14.

5. William J. Bausch, *Storytelling The Word* (Mystic, Connecticut: Twenty-third Publications, 1996), p. 145.

Lighting Of The Fourth Advent Candle

Leader: Scripture Reading — Isaiah 9:2-6

Leader: This candle we light today reminds us of the light of Joy the prophets had in their expectation of a Messiah who would bring good news to the world.

People: Glory be to God.

Prayer

Almighty God, giver of all good gifts and creator of everything that is, we worship thee and sing praises to thee because of the gift of thy Son in whom we are created in thine own image.

We thank thee, O God, for the gift of Christmas, for we know that since that night so long ago nothing has ever been the same. We thank thee for the coming of thy Son into the world and the Good News of his birth, his life, his words, his death and resurrection, and his call to come and follow him.

And we pray that because of this Christmas our lives would once again be touched by him. May it cause us to be more joyful, more helpful, more generous; may our lives take some new roads because we have come near to Bethlehem.

May Christmas this year shine its light upon us in some new ways, and may the light of Christ be seen all over the world. Because of that light may there be no darkness in our lives. May it shine along the roads we follow.

Give us faith, O God — faith in thee and in thy Christ and in the victory of thy Kingdom.

Bless our sick and sorrowful, and bless all the world for it is in his name we pray. Amen.

Looking At Our Chrismons:
An Angel

I am so glad to see each of you today. I'm glad you have come to worship on this Sunday in Advent. And who can tell us which Sunday in Advent this is? That is correct. This is the Fourth, or last, Sunday in the Advent season.

Do all of you remember what a Chrismon is? It is a Christ-monogram. It is a symbol which tells us something about Jesus Christ.

Today the Chrismon I want us to look at is this angel. We have several of these on our tree. Remember that the angel of the Lord came to Mary and told her she was going to have a baby, and he would be great. He would be God's Son.

Then, later on in the story, after Mary and Joseph arrived in Bethlehem, the angels came to the shepherds and told them about Jesus being born in Bethlehem. The angel said to them, "I bring you Good News of a great joy, which will come to all people, for unto you is born this day in the city of David a Savior, who is Christ the Lord. This will be a sign for you. You will find a babe, wrapped in swaddling cloths, lying in a manger." And the shepherds left their flocks and went into town to find the baby.

When you see this angel think about the Good News the angels brought to the shepherds, and not only to them. This is also Good News for each one of us.

Let's have our prayer. Thank you, Father, for the Good News about your Son and our Savior, Jesus Christ. Amen.

The Old Shepherd

Angels visit me all the time.

So the night the angels came to me out in the field, it sure wasn't the first time. That night, I was out in the field, a little ways apart from the other shepherds, tending my flock. Well, my grandson thinks it's *his* flock, but he's barely big enough to see over their heads. Anyway, an angel came and told me that the Son of God was being born in Bethlehem. That's where I lived all my life! The Son of God was being born there? I had to ask some questions, like, why Bethlehem, and which angel are you? It was a voice I hadn't heard before.

The angel didn't answer my questions — just touched my cheek and turned my face toward the East and said there was a huge star. Funny, none of the others had mentioned seeing it. I realized the angel wanted me to go toward that star and I would find the Christchild. Being blind, I listened carefully to the sounds in the sky, and after a while I could clearly hear where the star was. There was a lovely hum in that direction. I figured out that it was the sound of the angel's wings strumming the night air. I called for my grandson to bring the flock, and we started after the sound.

"Bring the rest, old man," the angel ordered me.

Well, that stopped me. They wouldn't listen to me. I'm old, I'm blind. The last time I told them an angel had spoken to me, they threw mud at me. Perhaps if I could get one of the younger men to believe me, he could persuade the others. I asked my grandson to lead me back toward where I could hear them talking. As we got closer I made out what they were saying. It amazed me. They were terrified.

This was amazing because it meant *they* had heard the angel, too, and seen the star. So I should have no trouble getting them to go with me to Bethlehem to find the child. That's what I thought, anyway.

"Walk all the way back into town? What about wolves? And what stable are we supposed to go to? What if we can't find the child, old man? We'll look like fools!"

What they weren't saying was, they were scared. So be it. But for me, there was only one choice.

"Fine," I said, "but we're going. This is my hometown, and I know exactly how to find the child." I didn't, but the angels and my grandson would lead me. "We're going. If anybody wants to come, this is the way. We're going to the newborn Messiah." And off we went.

It was chilly that night, I remember. But we didn't feel it much. I had to hurry along to keep up with my grandson. He kept skipping ahead and then running back to tell me about the star, or to let me know how many angels were leading us now. Every so often, I heard the flurry of an angel hovering at my shoulder. "Keep going, old man. You can make it."

All of a sudden, my grandson grabbed my hand and stopped me. "Grandpa!" he said, "Grandpa, they're coming!" I listened: yes, the others were coming! Feet scuffing across wet grass, muffled voices, sheep bleating softly to reassure each other.

I knew it. I knew they would come. If I could find the child, old blind me, they must have figured anyone could. Now here we are, in the presence of the baby King.

You see? Anyone can listen for the quiet hum of the angels' wings. Anyone can find this stable.

They Came Together In Bethlehem:
The Simple Shepherds —
And The Lamb Of God

Perhaps some of you remember a story written by Bret Harte called "The Luck of Roaring Camp." It was the story of a mining town. It was a rough place, with the roughest kind of people living there. There was only one woman who lived there among those miners. And she died giving birth to a baby.

The miners did not know what to do with him, so they put him in a box layered with old rags. They knew the box was not good enough for him, so one of them traveled to a distant town and bought a cradle for him. Then another decided the rags were not clean enough for him, and he traveled far away to buy something better. Then they all realized the house he was living in was dirty, so they cleaned it. They also had to clean up themselves because they held this baby. They also had to quit fighting and make less noise out in the street so he could sleep.

Over a period of time Roaring Camp was completely changed by the birth of this child, and so were those dirty, profane men who lived there. They were changed by a child.[1]

That is the kind of thing we see taking place in the dirty little town of Bethlehem.

Who are they that receive the news of the Savior's birth from the angels, and then come into town to see this great thing that has happened? It is the shepherds, of all people. Why the shepherds? What are they doing there?

We have been thinking together throughout this Advent season about the theme, "They Came Together In Bethlehem." Tonight we turn our thoughts to "The Simple Shepherds — And The Lamb Of God."

Centuries before the birth of Christ the prophet Isaiah had written about the coming of the Messiah. We had read for us earlier those words about this Messiah who would be despised and rejected, "a man of sorrows, and acquainted with grief." Isaiah writes that he has borne our infirmities, our griefs, carried our sorrows, was wounded for our transgressions, and was bruised for our iniquities. Then he tells us, "He was oppressed, and he was afflicted, yet he opened not his mouth; like a lamb that is led to slaughter, and like a sheep that before its shearers is dumb, so he opened not his mouth." This Messiah, according to Isaiah, was like a lamb. He would be the Lamb of God.

The Jews had for centuries valued the place of a lamb. For one thing, they would offer lambs for a sacrifice to God. Also they would place upon a lamb all their sins. Then they would take the lamb out into the wilderness and leave it, where it would die, along with their sins.

It is striking then that when John the Baptist saw Jesus at the Jordan River he said of him, "Behold, the Lamb of God, who takes away the sin of the world."

Tonight we think about the birth of Christ. And we see coming together in Bethlehem those simple shepherds and the Lamb of God.

Why shepherds, though? Why, of all people, did it have to be shepherds? Shepherds were not thought well of in those days, even though David, Israel's greatest king and national hero, had been one of those shepherds from Bethlehem. Shepherds were outcasts. They were despised and thought to be dishonest. Often they would let their flocks feed on other people's lands.[2]

Yet the angel of the Lord appeared to these shepherds with "the good news of great joy which will come to all the people." It was given to them. Saint Luke tells us, "When the angels went away from them into heaven, the shepherds said to one another, 'Let us go over to Bethlehem and see this thing that has happened, which the Lord has made known to us.' "

Do you want to know why the Good News came to such people? I can tell you why. Because God wanted to show that while Caesar Augustus, the emperor of Rome, had the power to force peace upon the empire, and Quirinius, the governor of Syria, was there to enforce peace, God would give the news of the Prince of Peace to the lowest kind of people because the Messiah was being born in the lowest kind of place.

So there we see coming together in Bethlehem the simple shepherds and the Lamb of God.

Put yourself in this great event tonight and make it real for you. Do what these shepherds did.

I

First, the shepherds came to the manger to find him. It was the shepherds who came looking for the Lamb of God.

Saint Luke writes, "And they went with haste, and found Mary and Joseph, and the babe lying in a manger."

The shepherds knew this was important, and they had a sense of urgency about it.

Sometimes we are in danger of missing this. It is easy for us to get swept along by all that is going on around us, and forget what it is we are really looking for at Christmas.

A man took his little girl to see that great parade following the inauguration of the President of the United States. As they stood there waiting, the girl kept wanting her father to buy her a hot dog from a vendor back over on the sidewalk. Finally, they pushed back through the crowd to buy the hot dog, just as the President came down the street. They missed him in this only time they would have the opportunity to be that close to him.

A seventh grade boy went with his class on a trip to Washington, D. C. When he returned home his parents were anxious to hear all about the trip. They asked him what he liked best out of all the things he had done. He thought a minute and said, "The pillow fights on the train."

A few days after Christmas Saint Peter was letting a line of men through the pearly gates. He was questioning each one. Among other questions, he asked each to state his I.Q. One said, "Mine was 191." Saint Peter asked, "What kind of work did you do?" The man answered, "I was a rocket scientist." Saint Peter waved him on in, and said to the next, "What was your I.Q.?" The man replied, "It was 172." When Saint Peter asked his line of work, he said, "I was a biochemist." Saint Peter waved him on through, and asked the next his I.Q. The man replied, "It was 47." Saint Peter looked at him and said, "Was that Tickle Me Elmo doll really worth it?"

Sometimes we miss the point of Christmas. When that happens it becomes empty and meaningless.

One Christmas morning a little boy sat by the tree in the middle of wrappings, presents, and gifts. He had a bewildered look on his face as he said, "Is that all there is to it?"

When we miss the point of Christmas, to the extent that it becomes empty and meaningless, then life becomes empty and meaningless.

The shepherds knew they came to the manger for one thing — to find this child which had been born.

II

Second, the shepherds shared what they had heard about him. It was the shepherds who heard about the Lamb of God and shared what they had heard.

Saint Luke writes, "And when they saw it they made known the saying which had been told them concerning this child; and all who heard it wondered at what the shepherds told them."

The shepherds knew this was important, and they had a sense of urgency about telling it.

Sometimes we are in danger of missing this. It is easy for us to forget this is the wonderful Good News we have received. And we have received it for one reason, to share it.

One night there were several babies born in a hospital. The maternity waiting room was crowded with fathers and families. At one point the nurse came to tell one man he had a set of twins. He said, "Isn't that something? My favorite ball team is the Minnesota Twins!" After a while the nurse came back and told another man he had a set of triplets. He said, "What a coincidence. I work for the 3M Company!" Those in the room noticed another expectant dad slump down in his chair. He had a sick look on his face.

Someone asked him what was wrong. He said, "I teach at a high school, and I am the faculty advisor for the 4-H Club!"

Here is a danger for us — that we settle down in our living with no compelling joy and no sense of urgency about sharing and living the meaning of our faith and the Good News that the Christ child has been born.

A preacher I know wrote in his church's newsletter about being at a high school basketball game. He was sitting with another preacher who suddenly laughed out loud. He said to him, "What's so funny?" The other preacher replied, "You see that lady over there jumping up and down and screaming at the referee? She is one of my members. She has a weak heart and is not able to come to church. Isn't it funny that she is able to be here and participate with vigor?"[3]

Do not lose the sense of urgency about the coming of Christ and the sense of urgency about sharing your faith.

The shepherds knew they had something to share. It was the Good News they had been given about his birth.

III

Third, the shepherds returned praising God for him. It was the shepherds who returned to their flocks giving thanks for the Lamb of God.

Saint Luke also tells us, "And the shepherds returned, glorifying and praising God for all they had heard and seen, as it had been told them."

They also knew this was important, and they had a sense of urgency about praising God for him.

Sometimes we are in danger of missing this. Now that you have come to Christmas, to Bethlehem, where all things come together, do not forget as you go away from it to praise God for all you have heard and seen.

We thank, worship, praise, and serve God because everything comes together in Bethlehem. Life and the meaning of it, faith and the basis of it, joy and the reason for it — all come together in Bethlehem.

There in Bethlehem we come together with a young couple and simple shepherds and the Lamb of God.

Back in the early '80s one of our churches in Atlanta decided to have a live manger scene. They made all their preparations and arranged to borrow some animals from the petting zoo at Stone Mountain. But it was one of those years when we had bitter cold weather and zero temperatures. So the church called off the live manger scene. But it was Christmas Eve, and they did not know what to do with the animals. They decided to divide them up among their members. One man took home, much to the dismay of his family, three sheep and one donkey. His wife thought he was one. He put them out in the garage.

Late that night he tried to sleep, but could not because he was worried about his animals. He went out to see if they were okay. Because of the cold he tried to put blankets on the sheep and a sleeping bag on the donkey. He went back out there later to check on them, and discovered the donkey had eaten half of the blanket. Maybe his wife was right.

Finally came the dawn, and he went to check on them again. And this time when he opened the door he saw not three sheep, but four. A lamb had been born early Christmas morning. He stood there looking at it in disbelief, and then he said out loud, "They called Jesus the Lamb of God. Behold the Lamb of God who takes away the sin of the world."[4]

One year when we had our own "Walk Through Bethlehem" we re-created the town and the stable area. I played the part not of a shepherd, but a goatherd. I had these two goats standing with me near the gates of town. One night I looked up and saw coming along the street one of our youth with a lamb over his shoulders. For a moment there I thought I saw young David, the shepherd, coming through Old Bethlehem with the Lamb of God. My heart was filled with joy as I remembered those words, "Behold the Lamb of God who takes away the sin of the world."

In Bethlehem we come together with the Lamb of God.

Thanks be to God!

1. James W. Moore, *Christmas Gifts That Always Fit* (Nashville, Tennessee: Dimensions For Living, 1996), p. 75.

2. R. Alan Culpepper, "The Gospel Of Luke," *The New Interpreter's Bible, Volume IX* (Nashville, Tennessee: Abingdon Press, 1995), p. 65.

3. Phil Demore, "The Bridge," First United Methodist Church, Gainesville, Georgia, December 11, 1996.

4. I am indebted to Greg Porterfield, Pastor of First United Methodist Church, LaGrange, Georgia, for this story.

Lighting Of The Christ Candle

Leader: Scripture Reading — Isaiah 53:1-7

Leader: This candle we light today is the Christ candle. It reminds us that Jesus Christ, God's son, has come to bring God's joy, salvation, and peace to the world.

People: Joy to the world, the Lord is Come!

Prayer

O God, our Father, as we gather here tonight there is a sense of wonder which still comes over the world on the eve of the birth of thy Son and our King.

And it is our prayer that none of us have grown too old, too mature, too wise, too cynical, or too tired to sense it.

So, we bow our heads as children, thy children. And we open our hearts and lives so that the one who comes to us will find a place to live in us.

We know he is our great need. We still need him. And we need Christmas. We need what it means and what it does, the hope it offers even to folks like us.

O God, the whole world needs Christmas and the hope it offers, because the whole world needs Christ, the hope of the world.

And we pray tonight that the Good News of the Savior's birth will be heard all across pastures where shepherds watch, on dusty roads by travelers, in small towns by shopkeepers and homemakers, in cities by tycoons and executives and slum-dwellers, garbagemen and policemen and policewomen, heads of state and prisoners and people like us: "Glory to God in the highest, peace on earth, goodwill to men."

For we pray in his holy name and for his sake. Amen.

Looking At Our Chrismons:
A Star

Good evening, girls and boys. This is it. It's Christmas Eve. This is what we have been waiting for. This is the night.

All during Advent we have been looking at our Chrismons. A Chrismon is a Christ-monogram. They remind us of something about Jesus Christ.

The one we look at tonight is a star. Look at our tree and you will see several of them. They remind us of the night Jesus was born.

When the shepherds were out in the fields, they heard the singing of the angels. They went up to Bethlehem and found the baby.

Then later, we are told, wise men came from the east. They were kingly teachers. They had followed the light of the star a long way. They followed that light all the way to Bethlehem. We do not know how long the journey took. It was several days at least. They followed the star until it came to rest over the place where Jesus was lying in the manger. The light of the star pointed to the place where he was.

In Bethlehem there is a church built over the place where Jesus is said to have been born. In the basement where the stable was there is a large gold star on the floor at the place of Jesus' birth. It is a reminder that the one born there is the Light of the world.

Let us pray. O God, we thank you for your Son Jesus, the Light of the world. May he shine in us. Amen.

The Innkeeper

Nothing about my life has been what I planned. I married a man a lot older than me, but we actually fell in love. He ran a busy inn right in the middle of one of the Roman tax centers. You might know of it — Bethlehem? Anyway, we were happy for a couple of years. Then my husband died. It about killed me. I decided that love was not for me, and I've managed fairly well without it. Wished we'd had a child, though. At least I still had the inn.

That one year at tax time there were extra crowds because of the comet everybody was coming to gawk at. I was full up, every room. One night, about the time I was going to bed, I hear a banging on the door. There stands this grimy, worn-out looking young man, says he wants a room.

"There ain't a room in this whole town, mister, lots of luck." I look past him and I see this young girl sitting on a donkey, and she is about nine months pregnant. "Look," I says, "I'm really sorry, but my place is full. Unless you want to sleep in the stable, you're out of luck." It was a *joke*.

But this man says, "All right, it's better than sleeping on a donkey's back."

He was serious, God help him. So I fixed them up in the stable. It's just a shed, really, but they seemed glad to have it. He said his name was Joseph and his little wife's name was Mary. I asked her when she was due and she sighed and said, "Tonight, any minute. The pains began an hour ago."

I went to look in on Mary a little while later, and Joseph was right at her side, patting straw up around her, stroking her hair. I had never seen a man so determined to help his wife give birth. And there she was about to deliver, and she was singing to calm *him* down. I swear, I'd forgotten how it was with young love like that. I left them some bread and a little wine and went inside. But I couldn't stop thinking about it, being in love and having your life ahead of you. I felt like that once.

Later on, in the middle of the night, there's Joseph at the door again, and he says Mary needs help. I think, "Do I need this?" but I went anyway. The baby was coming, and Mary being a first-timer didn't know what to do. So I talked her through it. Talked her poor husband through it, too. And then the baby was there. A boy, pretty little thing. I held him while his mother rested. When I handed him to her, she said, "Your name is Emmanuel ..." and it sounded like she said, "You are the son of God." I didn't know what she meant, exactly.

But there *was* a gift from God that night. I saw it in their little family. That young couple was starting out on a hard road, but they were full of hope. And love. That baby was their beginning. After my husband was gone, and I decided I'd never love again, I died some every day. But this baby boy, with his sweet mother and solemn father, made me believe there was still a chance, maybe even a tough old goat like me could hope, and love.

A crowd gathered around that stable. I knew what they'd find in that sweet little face, in that baby Jesus. Something had been born that night for me, too. It was a new heart, filled again with hope and love and life.

They Came Together In Bethlehem:
The Three Kings —
And The King Of Kings

A wealthy couple went on a trip to Hawaii. One afternoon the wife went down to the beach. After a while her husband walked down to the beach. He saw a group of people there trying to help someone. He realized it was his wife. He ran up to them and said, "What are you doing?" They replied, "We're giving her artificial respiration." He said, "Artificial nothing. Give her the real thing. We can afford it!"[1]

When we read about those three mysterious men from the East we need not be concerned about their long journey, their missing work at home, the expensive gifts they brought with them. They could afford it all. There was nothing artificial in who they were, what they did, or what they brought with them.

All through the Advent season we thought together about the theme, "They Came Together In Bethlehem." We come now to the end of the Christmas story, and today we will look at "The Three Kings — And The King Of Kings."

Centuries earlier the prophet Isaiah had written about the coming Messiah: "Of the increase of his government and of peace there will be no end, upon the throne of David, and over his kingdom, to establish it, and to uphold it with justice and with righteousness from this time forth and for evermore. The zeal of the Lord of hosts will do this."

Then, in Matthew's Gospel we have this account of the visit to Bethlehem by those who came to see this King. We see coming together in Bethlehem the three kings and the King of kings.

Finally come the wise men. We call them kings. But we are not exactly sure about what they were or who they were.

The Greek word for them is *magi*. It can mean "wise men," or "astrologers," or "magicians."[2] They may have been kings or princes. But they were at least some combination of royal priests who studied the stars. William Barclay, in his Bible commentary, says they were "teachers of Persian kings" and men "of holiness and wisdom."[3]

Matthew tells us these wise men came from the East to the city of Jerusalem. When they got there they began to ask around, saying, "Where is he who has been born king of the Jews? For we have seen his star in the East, and have come to worship him."

Herod, the maniac king, heard about this, and he became afraid. He was fearful of any threat to his power. And anything that upset Herod upset all of Jerusalem, because no one knew what he would do next. He learns from the priests and the scribes that the Messiah was to be born in Bethlehem. So he calls the three travelers to him, and sends them out to find the newborn king.

Interesting, isn't it, that priests, scribes, Levites and Pharisees, and all the holy men of Israel were not even interested enough to go down to Bethlehem to find out for themselves? It is a trio of Gentile holy men who make the trip for them all.

So these three wise men leave the city to find the King. They had lost sight of the star there in the lights of the city, but they find it again. They follow the light until they see it has come to stop over the place where the child was, and "they were overwhelmed with joy." They went inside and found the Messiah, the Christ child, the King of kings.

What do you do when you go into the presence of a king? This was not just the potentate of a small country, but the long-awaited King of the Jews who would be the Messiah who ushers in the new age of God's Kingdom over all creation. What do you do in the presence of such a King?

As we begin to move away from Christmas we see in these three wise kings what all wise men and women do in the presence of the King of kings.

I

They were wise enough to kneel before him. That is the first thing to remember. They knew that was the appropriate response for them.

Saint Matthew tells us that when they came into the place where the child was "they knelt down." Everybody always knelt down in the presence of a king. It was just the thing to do.

I wonder, would you be willing to do that even now? Would you be willing to kneel before him?

That is always the appropriate response to Christmas, the coming of the King of kings, and his presence with us today.

William Sloane Coffin was the pastor at Riverside Church in New York for a number of years. In a sermon he preached there on this story of the three wise men he pointed out the truths we still find in it today: "That people come from afar and by many ways to worship Christ ... that no place is too lowly to kneel ... that as knowledge grows so too must reverence and love."[4]

We kneel before Christ from wherever we have come, wherever we are as an expression of our love for him and his ways. That is what Christmas calls us to do.

A man took his granddaughter to see a manger scene. As they looked at it he pointed out to her everything which was a part of the story — the animals, the shepherds, Joseph and Mary, the manger and the baby, the three wise men. Then he said to her, "And there's the light of the star, but I can't see where the star is." She replied, "You can't see how the light shines in unless you get down and look up."[5]

One of the kings of England had some of his friends come to a meal with him. When he came in the room they all stood up. He seemed a little embarrassed and said, "Oh, you're my special friends. I'm not the Lord, you know." One of the men replied, "Sir, if you were we would not stand. We would all kneel before you."

That is what you do in the presence of this King. I hope you are wise enough to kneel before him.

II

They were also wise enough to worship him. That is the second thing to remember. They knew that was the appropriate response for them.

Saint Matthew tells us when they came into the place where the child was they not only knelt, they also "worshiped him." Some translations say they "paid him homage." Everybody always paid homage to a king. They often worshiped the king. It was the thing to do.

I wonder, would you be willing to do that even now? Would you be willing to pay him homage, to worship him?

That is always the appropriate response to Christmas, the coming of the King of kings, and his presence among us today.

We worship Christ because we accept his kingdom and his ways. That is what Christmas calls us to do.

Saint Augustine wrote these words: "It is love that asks, that seeks, that knocks, that finds, and that is faithful to what it finds."[6]

To worship Christ, to pay homage to him, is to be faithful to who he was and is, how he lived, what he taught, what he did in his life, death, and resurrection.

Do we not worship Christ most faithfully when we pay him the homage, the honor of imitation?

I saw in a television documentary the story of Father Colby, a Catholic priest in Poland. The Nazis discovered that he had been hiding Jews and protecting them. They arrested him and sent him to one of their death camps. One day someone escaped from the camp, and the Nazis decided that ten people would die because of it. One of the them they selected was a Polish Army sergeant. He begged that he be spared because he had a wife and several children. Father Colby stepped forward and volunteered to take his place. He gave his own life. It was said the camp was filled with light because of what he did.

There was a report on the evening news about a KKK rally in Ann Arbor, Michigan. Another group was there protesting against them. The two groups began shouting at each other. Then suddenly those protesting the Klan turned on a Klan member who got too close to them. They threw him down and began beating him with sticks. But something happened which was unexpected. A black woman named Kesha Thomas threw herself on the man and protected him with her own body. The other people walked away in silence.

Here are two examples of people willing to worship Christ, to pay him homage, not just by words, but by their deeds. They gave him the highest honor, which is imitation.

That is what you do in the presence of this King. I hope we are wise enough to worship him.

III

They were also wise enough to offer gifts to him. That is the third thing to remember. They knew that was the appropriate response for them. Saint Matthew tells us when they came into the place where the child was they not only knelt and worshiped him, they also opened "their treasures" and "offered him gifts, gold and frankincense and myrrh." Everybody always brought gifts to a king. It was the thing to do.

I wonder, would you be willing to do that even now? Would you be willing to bring him gifts?

That is always the appropriate response to Christmas, the coming of the King of kings, and his presence with us today.

We give gifts to Christ because we know he is God's gift to us. That is what Christmas calls us to do.

Love for Christ and his kingdom always calls us to give whatever is needed.

A man went into a pet shop to buy a bird. He was looking at several, which were all inexpensive. Then he saw one which cost several hundred dollars. When asked why the difference, the clerk said it was because this bird could talk. The man bought the bird and took him home. But the bird said nothing. The next day he went back to the shop and told them. He was told he needed to buy a ladder for the bird. He bought it and took it home, but the bird said nothing. The next day he went back to the shop and was told he needed to buy a mirror. He bought it and took it home, but the bird said nothing. The next day he went back to the shop and was told he needed to buy a swing. He bought it and took it home, but the bird said nothing. Late that night the bird took a downturn. The next day the man went back to the shop, and told them the bird did talk just before he died. The people in the shop asked, "What did he say?" The man replied, "He said, 'Don't they sell birdseed down at that store?' "

Love calls us to give whatever is needed. It is our love for the King of kings that calls forth from us the very best we have to give to him. And it calls us to give him our lives — all that we are, all that we have, all that we ever hope to be.

That is what you do in the presence of this King. I hope we are wise enough to give him the best gifts we have.

Kneeling before him, worshiping him, giving him our best gifts will bring us together with him in Bethlehem. And when we come together in Bethlehem with the King of kings all of life is set in order. It comes together. No matter what happens we will serve him, and we will know that he is with us.

This time between Christmas and Epiphany is called Christmastide, or the Christmas season. Sometimes we refer to the twelve days of Christmas. Epiphany is the day the church has long observed as the time of the visit of the wise men to the Christ child.

There is a song we hear called "The Twelve Days Of Christmas," which most of us know as being an old English folk song. You remember, "On the first day of Christmas my true love gave to me ..."

Father William J. Bausch gives us the story of that song in his book, *Storytelling The Word*. He writes that the song was composed by two Catholic Jesuits in sixteenth century England. By then the Catholic Church and the Catholic faith had been outlawed in England. Death and imprisonment were the punishments for being Catholic. But two Jesuits wrote a song of hope for all Catholics in England. And they sang it to bolster their faith and commitment in a difficult time. Here is the real meaning of that song:

> *"Twelve drummers drumming" were the twelve beliefs*
> *outlined in the Apostles' Creed.*
> *"Eleven pipers piping" were the eleven apostles, minus*
> *Judas.*

"Ten lords a-leaping" were the Ten Commandments.
"Nine ladies dancing" were the nine choirs of angels.
"Eight maids a-milking" were the Beatitudes.
"Seven swans a-swimming" were the seven sacraments
of the Catholic Church.
"Six geese a-laying" were the six precepts of the
Church.
"Five golden rings" were the first five books of the Old
Testament, the Pentateuch.
"Four calling birds" were the four Gospels.
"Three French hens" signified the three gifts the wise
men brought.
"Two turtle doves" meant the Old and New Testaments,
for the Spirit, the dove, inspired both.
"A partridge in a pear tree" is Jesus Christ who reigns
victoriously from the cross.[7]

So, on Christmas Day my true love, God, gave to me a partridge in a pear tree, his son, Jesus Christ. And he is why we come to Bethlehem, and come together with him. And he is why everything comes together in Bethlehem. We know he is with us no matter what, and that no matter what he will reign forever.

Thanks be to God!

1. James W. Moore, *Christmas Gifts That Always Fit* (Nashville, Tennessee: Dimensions For Living, 1996), p. 11.

2. M. Eugene Boring, "The Gospel Of Matthew," *The New Interpreter's Bible, Volume VIII* (Nashville, Tennessee: Abingdon Press, 1995), p. 140.

3. William Barclay, *The Gospel Of Matthew, Volume 1* (Philadelphia, Pennsylvania: Westminster Press, 1975), p. 26.

4. William Sloane Coffin, *Living The Truth In A World Of Illusions* (San Francisco, California: Harper & Row, 1985), p. 19.

5. Lamar J. Brooks, "... And On Earth, Peace," *Award Winning Sermons, Volume 3* (Nashville, Tennessee: Boardman Press, 1979), p. 33.

6. Susan Newman Hopkins, "What Love Demands," *Pulpit Digest*, March-April, 1992, p. 5

7. William J. Bausch, *Storytelling The Word* (Mystic, Connecticut: Twenty-third Publications, 1996), p. 203.

Lighting Of All The Candles

Leader: Scripture Reading — Isaiah 9:7

Leader: These candles we light today, after Christmas remind us to keep the light of Christ burning in our hearts through all the days ahead.

People: Amen.

Prayer

Almighty God, our Heavenly Father, who is the great creator of all that is and who dared to bend low in the coming of thy Son Jesus Christ, we bow before thee today.

We rejoice in the glad tidings of the Savior's birth. And we pray that we would be protected from the desire to get over Christmas and pack Jesus neatly up and put him away until next year, for Christmas is not even a week old and some of us are weary with it already.

Protect us, O God, from such weary living. Put a new song of joy in our hearts. For truly our lives have been blessed of thee. And we thank thee for thy graciousness toward us, for all the gifts we have received from thee and for all the gifts of love and friendship which others have shared with us.

We thank thee for this old year that is fading away and for the new year that is dawning. Into this new year may we take something of Christmas with us.

Bless those of our church family and community who have special problems. Be with those who are sick and in sorrow. Help them and be the Great Physician for them.

Bring some sense of hope, peace, and goodwill to this earth, and may we find those things in thy well-beloved Son, for we pray in his name. Amen.

Looking At Our Chrismons:
A Crown

Good morning. I hope all of you had a wonderful Christmas.

Here we are now on the Sunday after Christmas. We have come through the Advent season. Then we came to Christmas Eve and Christmas Day. And now Christmas is here. We celebrate the birth of our Savior, Jesus Christ. He is our newborn King.

We are told that when he was born among those people who came to see him were three wise men from the East. We talked about them on Christmas Eve, remember? They followed the light of the star all the way to the place where Jesus was born.

When they found him they fell down on their knees and worshiped him. Then they gave him gifts. They brought to him gold, frankincense, and myrrh. These were very expensive gifts. They were the kind of gifts you would give to a king.

He was a king, the newborn king of the Jews. He is still our king today. That is why we have this crown on our tree. It helps us remember that Jesus is our king still today.

Do you know what a king does? A king is a ruler. His people do what he says. He is their leader.

So to say Jesus is our king means we live the way he wants us to live. He is the one we worship and serve. This is why we celebrate his birth. This crown helps us remember these things.

Let us pray. Father, thank you for sending your Son to rule our lives. Amen.

The Wise Man

The arrangement was simple. The group of astrologers had come to Judea seeking the King of the Jews. King Herod wanted to be spared the bother of hunting for him. Herod wanted us to save him some time.

I knew that the child-king of Israel was to be born in Bethlehem. I had been studying those prophecies and watching the night skies all my life. I was eager to find this royal one, to pay tribute to his authority. Jerusalem is quite a distance from my home in Babylon. But there was great interest in him even there, and not only among the Jews.

Herod summoned us under cover of night. "Tell me where the child is," he had said, "so I can go and worship him, too." His hands were clasped in front of him as though in prayer. He was eager, almost frantic to get to the child. Well, we were going to the child anyway; why not tell Herod where we found him? Besides, Herod had a certain ... reputation. It would not do to refuse him a favor.

Herod suggested we take suitable gifts to the little king — that was how he put it, "little king." That caught me — there was something sly in his tone. He showed us the gifts he had prepared. Gold, an appropriate gift for royalty, a sign of the riches awaiting the one to be enthroned. Frankincense, a symbol of divine blessing and protection. I recognized these gifts, of course; they were foretold by the prophet Isaiah. But the third was not right, not appropriate. Myrrh. A burial spice; one mixed it with aloes to prepare a corpse for the tomb. He handed it to me in its elaborately disguised golden box. "Find him for me. I am most eager." Herod was smiling.

All the way into Bethlehem it troubled me. Myrrh? Who gives myrrh to an infant? It was obscene. I remembered Herod's words — "the little king" — and the strange look in his eyes. With a jolt, I knew. The child was a rival sovereign. Herod meant to kill him.

We found the house in Bethlehem and presented our gifts. The child's mother was gracious, but when I handed her the myrrh, her eyes clouded. What did we see in the stars for her little boy, she asked silently. I was afraid I knew.

I had a dream the night after we visited the child. I saw a cross-road, one road familiar and well-traveled, the other beautiful but unknown and very crooked. As I stood trying to get my bearings and choose a route, a tall, muscular man appeared. He stood in the intersection, one arm raised as if to show me the way. He was gesturing toward the unfamiliar road. It was then that I noticed that his fist was clenched. I became curious; he seemed determined to hold that hand shut. I thought he must be concealing some treasure of great value — a rare gem or a gold coin. I grabbed his wrist in my hand and pried his fingers open. Inside was no coin, no ruby or diamond. His hand was empty. But his palm had a scar. A hole, as though it had been pierced through with a spike.

I awoke trembling. He was showing me the safe way home. I knew I must not go back to Herod. We left by an alternate route, leaving Herod frustrated, the child still alive.

I don't know what will become of that little boy. But the man from my dream lingers. The road I thought was familiar and safe would have meant certain death. But the way *he* showed me took me home. We walk it together in my dreams. He does not leave me. And, I think, he will not.